"Daddy!
...Can You Hear Me???"

By Patrice Lee

U. S. Copyright - June, 2014
4th Printing - March, 2016
Special Edition – April, 2018

Published by Leep4Joy Books, a Div. of Feinstein
Printed in the United States of America

Library of Congress Catalog
ISBN: 978-0-9837207-8-2

Edited by: Cathryn Williams and Chelynne Lee
Cover: Francesco Paolo Ardizzone

All scripture references are taken from the King James Version of The Holy Bible.

Send correspondence to: Feinstein & Associates, P. O. Box 48172, Oak Park, MI 48237

We present this book to our Pre-K Dads
as a complimentary gift from:
Detroit Public Schools Community District's
Early Childhood Programs Department
**2nd Annual Dad's Day in Pre-K
Fatherhood Conference & Workshop**
Thursday, April 19, 2018
Franchott R. Cooper, Ed. S., LMSW
DPSCD Early Childhood Supervisor

Daddy! . . .Can YOU Hear Me???

May this resource serve as that tool which leads to an open door for healing and reconciliation to commence between fathers and their children, restoring families to a state of wholeness; and may it continue within those families for generations. May those barriers preventing good communication between children and their dads be removed, to allow for quality time to be shared between them.

Daddy! . . .Can YOU Hear Me???

Endorsements

"The messages of faith, hope, healing and love have a powerful effect in Daddy, Can You Hear Me??? Of all the Leep4Joy Books, perhaps this is the one that will have the greatest impact upon families."
Dr. Jim Holley, Pastor
Father and grandfather

"This beautiful poetry is indeed, poetry that will reach millions of people, because it has reached me. I am deeply moved and touched by these beautiful poems."
Charles Hart
Bassist, songwriter, producer
Father, two young adults, 4 grandchildren

"*Daddy! Can You Hear Me???* will help men who are disconnected from their children. Through it you can gain insight into what your child may have experienced while you were apart. Use this book to help you think, process and act in ways that will help your child grow to become the person that he or she was meant to be. And you will grow through this process too."

John Fort
Male and Female Involvement/Parent Coordinator
Proud father of five young adults

"This book makes me appreciate my dad more; and makes me want to be a better son."

Andrew C., Teen/son of a "great dad"

"Patrice Lee has a strong message to fathers that I think every father should read. It doesn't matter if you have great relationships with your children or if those relationships are strained. Her writings will inspire and challenge. They will comfort and, in some cases, convict. I find her literary style engaging as well as thought provoking. I recommend this book to anyone with a heart. I was deeply touched by her presentation."

**Bobby Ray Ivory, Jr,
CEO of Ivory Coast Media
3 adult children**

"I believe, and I am thoroughly convinced that this book of poems is a game changer. It asks probing questions of the reader, as it introduces related scriptures for guidance, while eliciting a heartfelt and truthful response that only the reader can answer. We can lie to others (who may not always perceive the truth about us), but, we can never lie to our own spirit. Though absent from many homes, fathers still hold the position of head of the home as ordained by God. Let *Daddy! Can You Hear Me???* change your life."

**Raymond L. Ford, Elder, Lutheran Church
Husband, Father**

Table of Contents

Daddy!. . .Can YOU Hear Me???

Foreword

As president of the National PTA, I have observed many great dads involved in PTA and can say that it is not a coincidence that engaged dads are making a positive difference in the lives of their children. Our presence matters at home, at school and in the community.

Spending quality time with your son or daughter when they are young, not only makes a difference in their life, it adds substance and meaning to your life as a parent as well. This is especially true if you're a dad. Lee's poems encourage continual interaction between fathers and their children, while motivating non-engaged (or absentee) dads to take that initial step to become involved.

In *Daddy! . . .Can YOU Hear Me???* Patrice Lee gently nudges dads to get involved, and reconnect or stay connected with their children, as she presents real-life scenarios through conversational poetry in a non-threatening way.

You may not see the benefits of your time and involvement at first, but the seeds of greatness, confidence, and good character that you plant by being there, will certainly take root. And just like the bamboo tree that doesn't show signs of growth until many years after being planted, your child will one day grow up to make you proud.

My son is one of those examples. When I first began to volunteer at his school, he wasn't very excited to see me there. Over time, my presence was welcomed by him and his friends. And today, he and I have become a close, father-son team at many venues in, and throughout my professional career. Needless to say, I am proud of the man he has become.

Let this book *Daddy! ...Can YOU Hear Me???* help you on your path to becoming the great dad your child needs you to be. Connect with other dads along your journey, and encourage them to do the same.

Encouraging fathers to engage today for a better tomorrow,

Otha E Thornton Jr

Otha Thornton, President
National Parent Teacher Association

Preface

Although he was older - retired before I went to high school - he would play tag with us. Dad usually started the game of tag, but, run so fast we could never catch him to hit him back. He always got such a chuckle out of our frustration, for we never wanted to lose in such an easy game. And, of course, we always told our mom that he had hit us (started the game of tag), and how it wasn't fair, because we couldn't catch him. :)

Our dad loved fresh produce, poultry, fish and the purest of products, so we became health-conscious early in life. One of our weekly activities, as children, was to go to the "Eastern Market" and shop with him. He knew everyone, and had hunted on many of their farms. My dad never met a stranger.

Therefore, a market experience that might have taken the average shopper 45 minutes, usually lasted at least two hours. Did I mention, he would pick up fresh cider and eggs for his brothers and their families too, more often than not? Did I say? "He was a great dad." Not only was he a great dad, he was a great man.

13

Needless to say, my father lived a life of integrity, faith and faithfulness to God and his family. He loved Jesus and his family dearly.

Many children today are not fortunate enough to have a dad play an active role in their lives. And it is for those children that I write, hoping this book will touch the lives of fathers everywhere, and make a difference.

The message that I share in this book is a positive one, thought-provoking and sincere. Our children need a few good men to step up to the plate and play ball. You may not always hit the ball on the first pitch, and you may not hit a home run, but at least swing the bat and get an "A" for trying.

The rewards for your effort of becoming a great father and role model for your son or daughter are worth it. For if you teach your children how to swing the bat – how to live life – there's a strong possibility of them hitting a home run.

"Eastern Market" – is a Detroit Landmark known for its' fresh produce.

Introduction

"Fathers are critical to child development. Girls who feel rejected by their fathers often have a fear of abandonment and of commitment. They feel unworthy, unlovable. And too many boys grow up without someone to show them what it means to be a man." *

It is not a coincidence that some children and youth today are so full of anger, that they are unable to shed those feelings of rejection and unworthiness. To have the affirmation of a father could certainly change who that child is today, and greatly affect who they will become.

That is the reason why this resource was created for those dads who really do care about their children, but somehow their ability to have good communication has been interrupted. Those Dads just need a boost or a jumpstart, to rev them up, and to encourage them to keep on being great dads.

Thus, we write to you, and for you, to make a difference in the life of your young child, before he/she gets exposed to all of the distractions that don't mean them well. Somehow, somewhere, wherever you are Dad, if you aren't playing an active role in your child's life, for whatever reason, we hope that you will get matters in order; and (that you will) forgive, mend and heal, all at the same time. As you allow healing to begin, it will make room for all of your good intentions and desires to be (or to become) the best father you can be for your children to be fulfilled.

Ever wonder why a baby always calls your name first, after Mom has carried him (her) for nine months? No one can take your place Dad. ☺ You are the one they want and need. Babies get it! Babies understand the need to bond with you, because they had nine months to bond with Mom.

Let *Daddy, Can You Hear Me???* help you establish a stronger bond, and enhance your ability to have better communication with your children. You will find that the love you pour into your child is reciprocal.

Kudos to you, Dad, for taking time to read this little book. This resource, these poems were created just for you.

* Quote taken from: Irreplaceable: Why Fathers Matter, a documentary film, Focus On the Family, April, 2014.

Hey Dad, Which One Are You?

Some Dads are great fathers,
And some don't know what to do.
Some have confessed that they've missed it,
While others don't have a clue.

So what does it take to get your attention?

No matter how you look at it,
You're probably one of the four.
All we ask is that you strive to be the best dad
Nothing less, nothing more!

Daddy! . . .Can YOU Hear Me???

"Heart" to "Heart"

Daddy! . . .Can YOU Hear Me???

A "Heart to Heart" Conversation about Your Special Gift

Your child is God's gift to you. Each one, born with their own special talents or gift(s) will have dreams and desires of their own. Take the clam for example. The clam gives us pearls, but it must endure tremendous agitation before it can produce that beautiful pearl.

Consider your children to be as precious as the pearl. Like the pearl, children must be guided through the agitation of "living" life. With the right amount of structure and discipline, and the investment of quality time, you can expect your labor of love to yield tremendous results in each child.

Yes, children are a work-in-progress. They must be molded and shaped into the human being(s) that we want them to be. And it doesn't happen overnight. They are quite like the bamboo tree root that is planted in the ground for years before you see any signs of growth. Then, suddenly you have a very tall tree.

~

Daddy note: The reward is in knowing that you've done a great job, then seeing the end result.

A "Heart to Heart" Conversation:

About the Early Years

Everyone wants his dream to succeed, but every dream must go through a process in order to be realized. You must have a plan. The planning stage is followed by the execution stage, with many checkpoints or milestones along the way, until that goal is achieved.

During your child's early years, it might help to see your child as an extension of your vision, as a part of your dream team, with specific goals that you can work on together. One of your goals is to teach him basic life skills.

As you progress together, you will notice each little success. Encourage your child to work toward achieving or realizing specific goals each week, and watch him grow. His success is your success, for he just wants to know that you'll be there, to do life together with him until he can fly on his own.

~

Daddy note: Children look and long for heroes in their lives. They are very loyal people too. If you spend quality time with your child while he (she) is young, you will have a friend for life.*

*Children will look after you kindly when you are older.

Looking for My Hero

So many are crying, their voices lost in the wind.
Children are looking, grasping, longing for a
smile. . .or a hug;

With lost hopes and unspoken desires merely
Swept under – a rug.

Leaving brilliant minds – wandering,
Often destroying dreams and visions
Of the most creative kind.

Hey, I'm just looking for my **hero-o-o!**

Daddy note: Dad, can you call me sometime,
'cause I don't have your new phone number?

~

Will You Be My Hero?

Would you be my hero Dad?
Did you know that you're the one I adore?
I just want so much more than a
Than a quick hello, or sad good-bye

I want a lasting commitment
And for things to be different
Than they were before (before you went away).

~

Dad,

...Your name is more than a title to me

Dad,

Your name is more than a title to me, 'cause I really need you in my life. In your presence I feel safe, secure, free. Just can't imagine living my life without you. I'm trying hard to see my way through.

'Cause the times when you aren't here, sometimes I don't know what to do. Promise you'll be here, and that you'll never leave. So grateful for the friends I have, but, Dad you're the one I need.

Dad, I Need You!

Sometimes your job takes you away for a little while. But each time I see you, I greet you with a great big smile.

And when you're here, somehow I feel safe, (knowing I'm) not alone. Dad, I feel so happy, when you're at home.

It's that secure feeling I get when your hand is holding mine. The fun times we have together, rain or shine.

But, if for some reason I don't see you today, I want you to know how much I love you, and when I pray, I'll remember you.

That I'm doing things Dad, to make you proud of me. I'm getting good grades, ...I won the spelling bee, ...got down all by myself when I climbed that maple tree.

I learned to ride my bike with the handles turned back. Tryin' out for sports this year, might even run track.

Oh Dad, I'm going to do all I can (do) to be the best I can be. 'Cause all I want is for you to be proud of me.

25

Daddy Note: Dad, when you're not around, your children suffer, because there's no one, I repeat, no one who can replace a father's love. Is your child crying out for you?

Good Communication between
Father and Son

If you want your children to be happy, if you're hoping they'll learn to be content, they'll need you to be the example of happiness, and for you to show them what it is to be content. And they will follow your lead; for children simply mimic what they see their parents do.

"Dad, I love you!"

A *'Two-Way'* Conversation

Hey Son, Let's Talk!

I want you to know you're important to me
So let's sit down, and talk for awhile,
Just as soon as you are free.

Hey Dad,

It's been a while since we shared,
We've got some catchin' up to do.
There've been a lot of changes, especially at school.

So let's get together soon, just you and me.
Today looks pretty good.
How about 2 or 3?

Daddy note: **Keep the home atmosphere conducive to open and honest conversation.**

A Teenage Son in Need - Reaching Out:

"Dad Can I talk to You?"

Can I have a moment please?   I need to finish the conversation that we started a few days ago? I'm trying to understand what's going on with me.   But, no one seems to have the time to hear my earnest plea.   Dad, we've talked about this before.   But, it's different this time.   This time it's so much more. . .

Looking back: Thank you for your time today.   I believe I'm gonna make it.   And I can still hear your voice saying, "Son, it's going to be okay." Thanks Dad.

29

Hey Dad, You're Different

So glad you're different Dad;
You're not one to pretend.
You always keep your commitment.
On your word we can depend.

You're big and strong, and all that good stuff.
You always know how to handle things,
When things get a little tough.

It's not just about the toys and gifts,
Or the great things you do for me.
But, it's what I observe and see in you,
That help me strive to become a better me.

Love Note to Dad:

Dad – Thank you for protecting me from dangers I
know not of, and for shielding me from all that could
have been.

"Honor thy father and mother . . ." Ephesians 6:2a

Borderline Communication:

It's been a while since I've heard from you, Dad. I'd love to have a conversation with you; because every word you say is important to me. Later on today, do you think you'll be free?

~

Well Dad, though I haven't seen you for a while
But, when I think of you – I still smile.

~

Daddy, Can You Hear Me???

It matters that you know what's going on
That when you say you'll be there, you won't
leave me hangin' on. . .to your promises.

It matters that you keep your word,
And that you arrive on time,
Want you to be there Dad, to see me shine.

'Cause I need to know that I'm still your
Sweetie pie. I'm going to reach for the stars,
So I can touch the sky.

What I realize when you're away is
How much I miss hearing you say,
"How's Daddy's girl?" I love you Daddy!
Don't know where you've been.
All I know is, I can't wait to see you again.

And Dad, Can You Hear Me???

Oh Dad, can you hear me?
It's me, your energetic son.
I need to know I'm on the right track
And that you'll be there for me,
That someone's got my back.

I'd like to follow in your footsteps Dad, and
Let my wings unfurl;
Discover, invent, and patent my ideas
To make a difference in this world.

'Cause one day I hope to make you proud.

~

All I Needed was a Conversation
(from a son)

Dad- You were so serious and strong,
And the distance between us – long.
I needed you to show me that you care
For you to talk to me and share
The things I needed to know
So I could one day – grow,
Into the **man** I was meant to be.

What I needed was a conversation with you.

~

All I Wanted was a Conversation
(from a daughter)

Dad- You were so serious and strong,
And the distance between us – long.
I needed you to show me that you care
For you to help me prepare.
To tell me all the things I need to know
So that one day I could grow
Into the **woman** I was meant to be.

All I wanted was a compliment or two.

Dad Note: If you're not available, not interested, or just don't want to be bothered - please reconsider, because your children need you. Even if you're far away; you can Skype and talk as if you're right there.

~

(Just Some Things I Need to Know)

What I want to know is . . .
Was bullying a problem when you were little
Dad? And if it was, what did you do?
How did you handle it Dad?
Did they pick on you?

Sometimes they call me a bully,
But I'm just reacting to the things they say
And do.   Sometimes I'm the one that gets
bullied. So how can that be true?

The other thing I want to know is . . .
Did you have trouble with spelling?
Do you pronounce all of your words right?
These little things, well, they don't bother me
Because I study almost every night.

Dad, someone said, "Life isn't easy."
But, I wanna' know what you think.
Can it get any tougher than this?
Is that why teens - drink?

I'm having some real issues now – and they say my problem is . . .

"Dad,"
Do you think my problem is connected to "YOU?"

--- I'm just trying to figure this thing out.

No Communication

~ between father and child ~

There's no need to blame it on the baby's Momma –Even if it is her fault, can you talk it over? You may have to be the role model, Dad, so try to work it out! The children are observing and they are taking notes. It just takes one good man.

A good woman will submit to a good man when a man with good intentions takes authority. :) Good men take authority without showing anger.

Is there a good man in the house???

God's plan was for husbands and wives to love each other, for them to be fruitful, and for homes to be filled with love, children and laughter. His desire was for families to be together.

Jesus was the perfect example of love. Learn to love as He loves – "unconditionally." Walking in unconditional love can lead you to a place of perfect peace. And if you walk in complete forgiveness, you will be able to reconcile your differences and become whole again.

A Conversation -
I'd Like to Have with My Dad

I'd like to have a conversation with you dad.
Yep, it's me. I'm the one you never knew.
I was born some time after you left our Mom,
And suddenly I grew, and grew.

Now I'm old enough to understand,
That I had a father too. And the other children
I'd seen playing with their dads
Were considered a fortunate few.

I feel like I've really missed out,
On what seems like it could have been great
I just want to know if I'm almost twenty-one,
Is it too late???

There's still so much I don't know
Your kind advice I really could use.
I'm making so many decisions
Sometimes it overwhelms, to confuse.

The family says that time has flown
But, I can't say it has.
I'm trying to get over the fact that
I didn't have you today, or yesterday.
And (I've) no memories from the past.

If time, as they say, has really sped by
Then why can't I catch up?
It's been a long time now that I've been
waiting to talk to you.
I just wanna' know "What's up?"

"Daddy???"

I got questions Mom couldn't answer.
So may I bother you?
Please respond to my inbox message,
Especially if this is you.

Dad, I need you!
Why did you go away?
Is there something I can do?
Is there anything I can say?

Did you have to leave so suddenly?
When will you be coming back?
Everything's so different now,
And the house is such a wreck.

Oh, the things at the house are still in place,
It's our family that's all shook up.
How I'd love to look outside one day
And see your big old truck.

I guess I've asked enough questions,
Though I have so many more.
I just hope and pray that one day
You'll come strolling through that door.

Dad Note: When a dad leaves, it's the child who is left behind wondering what happened??? Children sometimes think that it's their fault when their questions about your absence remain unanswered. And sometimes they never get over it.

You never gave me a chance to tell you, but,

"I love you dad!"

Some Things are Too Difficult to Talk About

Daddy! . . .Can YOU Hear Me???

There are some topics that are just too difficult to mention, because they hurt so bad. Some things we can't explain, but, children still want to know about them. Sometimes they ask why.

Here's one of those things they ponder about - adoption. "Why was I adopted?" "Who is. . .? "What happened to my birth mom and dad?" "Where are my biological parents?" It's normal to want to know.

This next poem is dedicated to the child who hopes to one day meet his (her) biological mom or dad. May he (she) find peace in knowing that he (she) is loved. . .

(I was) Adopted
/Still Feeling Rejected – (after all these years)

I was young when my parents adopted me.
They said I was only three.
I wouldn't have known that I was adopted
Except they didn't look like me.
Dad, will I ever get to see you face-to-face?

Just want to know who I am,
Tried to find my biological mother too,
But, she passed some time ago.
I'm thankful for those who loved and cared for me,
But, I'm still struggling with this curiosity.

I've often wondered, "Does he know about me?"
"Did Mom say I was on the way?"
Or was I the result of a passing moment on the
cool of a pleasant day?
Maybe I'll recognize you, if I get to see your
face.

Perhaps I've already encountered you, but,
How would I ever know? And, if you saw me
To know me, would you let your feelings show?
Wonder if I'd recognize you, if I saw your face?

I've been looking for you, for a very, long time.
Can't believe it's you, I'm still trying to find,
But, it means that much to me;
And for me to know who you are.
For I've yet to see your chiseled face.

Could it be that you live in the same vicinity?
Around the corner, down the street, on the next
block? Or in the same neighborhood?
How I've longed for that special day,
Hoping to find you; there's got to be a way.

You're a lot older now and so am I.
A boomer is what they call **me!**
Dad, you've got to be close to eighty now.
Wonderin' if I'll ever have an opportunity,
If you're yet alive, to one day see your face.

'Got grandchildren now, and some are almost
Grown. Once they started coming,
I stayed a little closer to home.
Wanted to be a part of their reality.
Hoping one day your face they'll see.

Can't believe I'm still lookin', and still wonderin'
"Do I look like you at all?"
Or, maybe now that I'm older,
Perhaps I resembled you more when I was small.
I'm still trying to imagine who you are.

Your hair - a salt 'n' peppered grey by now.
I imagine you're quite the handsome chap;
Perhaps, you use a cane, or maybe you walk
Upright. Dad, is anyone looking out for you?
Do you drive when it rains?

Maybe you don't have to drive at all.
Or even need a car.

Until I get to see that chiseled face of yours,
Guess I'll always be wonderin' who you are.

"Dad," were you there when they adopted me???

Incarcerated

I'm incarcerated now
Not saying it's all your fault
But, if you had been around,
Maybe some of the things I did
I would've given more thought.

I've done some time here
And still have more time to do.
If you only knew - how much I needed you;
If only I could talk to you.

Maybe if we had talked
In my formative years when
I was two or three,
It might have set me on a
Different path - one of victory.

You were kind of busy then
Not sure what had you occupied.
But, if I'd known I had your approval
I would've been satisfied.

It seems like the streets kept calling me.

All I know is, I'd like to have
A better life; and to be free of
The chains that bind me.

And when I get out.
I'd appreciate any time you can give
For the path of life I chose,
Is not how I want to live.

And Dad, if you can't help me get through this
Please tell me someone who can.

Because I want to know
How I can be a better man.

~ Lookin' for someone to show me the way
'cause I'm tired of the streets. ~

Simply Trying to Communicate

(From a troubled teen)

"I've Got Something to Tell You"

I guess I'm angry, and didn't know it.
. . .Hurting, but try not to show it.
Confused, and disappointed too.

Can't control the way I feel,
Now I'm acting up at school.
Don't know what I'm gonna' do.

One minute I'm okay
The next minute I'm not.
"What's the matter?" They ask.

Can't stop "thinking" of **you!**

Do you think the two are connected?

It may not have worked out in the past, but don't stop trying to communicate. Keep trying. That's all you have to do. Children need to talk; parents do too.

Keep the communication going. The rewards may seem few, but, you're winning the battle against the odds when your children choose to talk to you. :)

Practicing good communication will cause any situation to improve. Sometimes it's just being kind or offering a kind word or two.

In this section, we provide different scenarios to help you improve your communication skills with your children.

A Dad's Phone Response to "Daddy, are you coming to pick me up today?"

"Your mom and I are going to have a talk. We've got a few things to work through. Daddy loves you. We're going to spend some time together soon, okay? Is Mom there?"

~

Hey Son (Daughter),

(A note from a dad with unusual work hours) "I love you, and I want to connect with you, as soon as my schedule will allow."

"I've been working extra hours, and you're asleep when I get home. I'm going to make it up to you. Hey son, 'want you to know I'm proud."

~

A Dad's Urgent Inbox Message to his Teenage Daughter:

"You've always been a daddy's girl; and we've always been able to talk. Did I see a picture of you on Facebook earlier today? Why don't we go for a walk?"

Note: Children will stay away from trouble if you teach them to keep the caution light on at all times, and to listen to the voice within.

A Daughter texting her Dad:

I know you've been trying to reach me.
I got your message sort of late.
Hope we can talk later today.
That would be really great.
~ and Dad said okay~
I have a lot of things to share.
Don't worry, everything's okay.
I'm making some important decisions Dad.
Want you to know, I'm on my way.

~

A Son reaching out to his Dad:

Dad, I've been trying to reach you. Tried to call you yesterday, but, I wasn't able to get through.

The number I dialed says the voice mail's full. So I sent you a text. I emailed you too. Did you get it? I want, ...**I need** to talk to you.

Things are not going so well, but I know I can talk to you. Thanks, Dad, for getting back with me.

~

Talk! And keep on talkin'. You'll reap all the benefits later, if you keep the conversations going, and take time to talk now.

Congratulations! You're making progress. :)

Hey Dad! I've Been Trying to Reach You

Hey Dad! I've been trying to reach you.
Did you get my text?
Found out what I was missing in my life.
It was "J - E - S - U - S!"

If you have a moment now,
I'd like for the two of you to meet.
He not only became my Friend, my Rock, my
Confidant, He pulled me off the streets.

Somehow I think you'll like Him
'Cause there may be some benefits for you
Man, I'd love to connect you to Him,
There's no tellin' what He will do.

Ps. I love you!

One Teen's Prayer

Dear Heavenly Father,

I'm thankful for this day
And for all that you've done for me.
For without you in my life Lord,
"Where would I be?"

Bless my Dad in all the things he has to do.
And since he's busy Lord, "May I talk to you?"
My friends don't understand me,
'Cause their dad's are with them continuously.

And when they ask me, "Are you okay?"
I tell them, "Sure, I'm fine."
But, You know how I feel inside,
'Cause You're here all the time.

Thank you for Your friendship Lord,
Without it, can't tell you what I'd do.
'Cause we have a special connection.
Nothing comes between me and You.

Thank you for letting me be your son (girl),
Nothing else matters right now.
Somehow, You make me feel special,
Like I'm your *only* child.

I love being in your presence.
I want to do what pleases You.
My biggest challenge is forgiveness.

Today, I'll let go of anger, bitterness,
Resentment, ...and if there's any hate - that too.

Though things haven't been perfect. . .
Please let dad know he's forgiven, and,
"Dad, I love you." :)

~

Text to Dad: "Dad! Do you think we can get
together soon? I'm not mad anymore."

Adopted, Self-Response – (I'm Okay now)

It's apparent Dad, I've been crying out.
It's something I had to do.
For I've found healing through my expression,
And consolation in (my) reaching out to you.

And I've realized in my search to find you
How blessed and fortunate I've been (I am).
For I've had two parents that have loved and
Cared for me since the tender age of ten.

Realizing now, how difficult parenting can be –
A whole lot to handle, quite a demanding task.
Perhaps you weren't ready for responsibility.
What I received was all one could've asked.

How selfish of me to keep looking for you,
Maybe you aren't quite ready yet.
And perhaps it is better I not know you,
Than to have wished we hadn't met.

Rejection, disappointment, misunderstandings
Were all wrapped into one big ball.
But, I met a friend that loves me so much;
Who helped me eliminate them all.

Without His love and compassion, honestly,
I don't know what I would have done.
It was Jesus, who healed my brokenness,
Now, I want to share Him with everyone.

Dad note: I was simply trying to communicate.

Daddy! . . .Can YOU Hear Me???

Teacher, ...

...and Promise-Keeper
(one who keeps his word)

Teach! Teacher, Teach!

...but, please don't lecture and please, please don't preach to your children.

Teacher, ...

As parent and teacher, try not to repeat too much, and know when it's time to back off. Too much repetition is a definite turn-off. :(

...and Promise-Keeper

Every promise you make to your child should be kept. So please make them sparingly.

Don't Wait!

Don't wait until it's too late
Or 'til someone's come and gone
You owe it to your children
To teach them right from wrong.

Let your children know that
Respect is not an option,
That there are consequences
For everything they do.

Someone has to do it.
Why shouldn't it be you?

~

I. . .Don't Feel Like a Teacher???

There is no better teacher than you. Besides, you get to enjoy the fruit of your labor when you give it your all, and you'll get most of the credit for a job well done.

Spending the early years with your babies and toddlers allows you to have the greater influence on your child's cognitive and core value systems, because you are your child's first and most important communicator of life, justice, of peace, and love.

So why not give them everything they need to be a well-rounded, productive citizen? Validate them every day, by letting them know when you are proud of them, and let them know they are loved.

Teach your children valuable lessons to help them grow into unselfish human beings. And Dad, when you make a promise, do all that you can to keep it, because they will have enough opportunities to be disappointed by others throughout life. On the next few pages you'll find more tips to help you succeed in some very critical areas. . .

Life Lessons: to share with your children

Tell Them Everything You Want Them to Know!

- Teach your children to be unselfish through serving others. They can learn this by volunteering for the senior members of the family, at home, church, school, etc. It's a good seed to sow in life, and will help them grow in many ways.

- Teach your babies to learn from their failures, by encouraging them to keep trying. Teach them to value life, to value self, and to have self-worth. Esteem them through words of praise.

- Teach them to respect self and others. Show them how to add value to the lives of others by speaking highly of them and encouraging them to speak positively about others.

- Help your children to know who they are as you nurture each step of progress with admiration and praise; and watch their confidence grow.

- Have you ever noticed how driven parents are to get their baby to walk? You can apply that same drive and energy to everything else you want your child to know. It should be that important to you, as it is for them.

And Dad, you'll have great peace if you do what the Word of God says. Here are a few things to keep in mind. As a Dad, and the head of your family, it's important for you to do the following:

"Seek ye first the Kingdom of God, and His righteousness, and all these things (whatever you have need of) will be added unto you" (Matthew 6:33).

"In all thy ways acknowledge Him, and He shall direct thy path" (Proverbs 3:6).

The Word also says in Isaiah 54:13 that those children who are taught of the Lord, shall have great peace.

Give your children a firm foundation. Teaching them the Word of God will help them go through the storms of life. And when the winds blow, they won't fall down. Here are some wonderful scriptures for parents and children to live by:

"Trust in the Lord with all thine heart, and lean not unto thine own understanding" (Proverbs 3:5). They need to know that they can stand on God's Word and trust Him.

Let them know that when you aren't around, they'll always have a friend in Jesus, and that He is on their side: "The Lord is on my side; I will not fear. What can man do unto me?" (Psalm 118:6).

65

Let them know what God says – that the Greater One lives in them: "*Greater is He that is in me, than he that is in the world*" (1John 4:4b) and "*No weapon formed against thee (you) shall prosper*" (Isaiah 54:17a)..

Constantly assure them of your love, but, teach them about God's unconditional love: "*. . .Let us love one another; for love is of God, . . .*" (1 John 4:7b).

Share with them that no matter what happens during the day, that God will keep them strong, because he promised to be, and is... "*God is our refuge and strength, a very present help in trouble*" (Psalm 46:1).

And, as it relates to bullies, let your children know that God's peace surpasses all: "*And the peace of God, which passeth all understanding, shall keep your hearts and minds through Christ Jesus*" (Philippians 4:7)

Getting Wisdom:

With all thy getting, get wisdom, for it is the principal thing. . .

Some Things You Need to Know. . .

. . .If you're waiting for the right time or the perfect time to get involved in your child's life, there's no time like – Now!

. . . If you're waiting for certain conditions to change, you may be the change you're waiting for. Take action today!

. . .If you're looking for something or someone to inspire you, you may have to inspire yourself. Then become an inspiration to others.

. . .If you're waiting for someone to apologize, you may have to initiate change by forgiving first. In order to move forward, you must forgive.

. . .If you want to experience relief from pain, you must release all the hurt, bruises and scar tissue from your past.

. . .Take the lead. Encourage yourself to be, or to become the best father you can be for your child. The rewards are great and lasting. And you'll find that the lessons you teach will have more rewards than you'd ever imagine.

Seek Wisdom and Understanding will follow:

Govern your affairs with wisdom; and ask God for wisdom when you don't know what to do. He will keep you from being bitter and help you avoid strife. He will strengthen you. He will help you. And He will uphold you (uplift you) with His righteous right hand. Isaiah's 41st chapter will encourage you and help you remain strong.

Words of Wisdom

There are many "words of wisdom" for fathers. You will find many of them in the book of Proverbs in the Holy Bible. There are 31 chapters, one for each day of the month.

Here's an example of what you'll find:

"Hear, ye children, the instruction of a father, and attend to know understanding. [5]Get wisdom, get understanding: forget it not... [6]Forsake her not, and she shall preserve thee: love her, and she shall keep thee. [7]Wisdom is the principal thing; therefore get wisdom: and with all thy getting get understanding. [8]Exalt her, and she shall promote thee: she shall bring thee to honor, when thou dost embrace her. [10]Hear, O my son, and receive my sayings; and the years of thy life shall be many" (Proverbs 4:1, 5a, 6-8, 10).

Dad note: Having, and exercising wisdom, can actually add years onto your life. As you live your life without strife, you will enjoy better physical health.

It's very difficult to be the best example for your son or daughter without a personal relationship with Jesus. So if you haven't made Jesus Lord of your life, why not today? You can do it by saying these words out loud:

"Dear Heavenly Father, I come boldly before the throne of Grace to repent of my sins. I ask you to cleanse me from all unrighteousness, and believe that you sent Your only Son, Jesus, that I might be free of sin. I believe He died on the cross and arose on the third day. Today I invite Jesus into my heart, and make Him Lord of my life. Thank you for saving me now, in Jesus Name, Amen."

Congratulations! Your decision to receive Jesus as Lord of your life is the best and most important decision of your life.

~

Did you know you can rely on God's Word and His promises to help you through life? I opened my Bible one day when I was almost ready to give up. But, the Lord was right there to encourage me. Through His Word, He let me know that I was never alone. These are the words He showed me; and the words came alive for me on that day:

"Fear thou not; for I am with thee: be not dismayed; for I am thy God: I will strengthen thee; yea, I will help thee; yea, I will uphold thee with the right hand of my righteousness" (Isaiah 41:10).

And He did just that. Now when I finished reading it, I knew without a doubt that God loved me. For His Word came alive for me on that day.

A Little More Wisdom:

If you haven't seen your son or daughter in awhile, you might open the conversation with "I love you son/daughter" or "I love you, man" or "Daddy loves you, sweetheart."

Children need hugs; and seldom turn down a loving embrace from a parent, no matter how long it's been since they've seen him. Hugs and embraces are usually welcome mats for reconciliation to begin.

If for some reason, others have not spoken kindly of you in your absence, you may want to open your channel of communication with what I call **"love notes."** When it seems that your best verbal conversation isn't getting you anywhere, or you're looking for a place to begin, **"love notes"** can serve as a gateway to open the door of communication.

In your **"love note"** you can begin to share things that you want your children to know, that can help them grow into a wonderful person, or anything positive about them that you'd like to share.

God desires for us to ask for wisdom, and He promised to give it to us: "If any of you lack wisdom, let him ask of God, that giveth to all men liberally..." (James1:5)

Daddy! . . .Can YOU Hear Me???

(Getting) a Fresh Start:

Sometimes in life you just need to start over again. And forget the past. Are you ready for a fresh start?

A Father's Promise

As a Father, I Promise Myself That. . .

- **I will** do more than be there for my child. I will play an active role in his/her life.
- **I will** do more than say I care. I will give my children a hand up when needed.
- **I will** do more than believe in their ability to accomplish a goal. I will take action, and be there to assist them when needed.
- **I will** do more than forgive the events and people of my past, including all hurts and failures too.
- Because forgiving helps me heal and forgetting helps me move on, and through. So **I will** forgive, put it behind me, and move on.
- **I will** do more than say it. **I will** do what must be done to be the great father that I was destined to be.

"I can do all through Christ who strengthens me."
Philippians 4:13

A Fresh Start for a #1 Dad

We're calling on you fathers,
Can't you hear your children's cry?
They don't want to know what happened,
Or to know the reasons why.

They're just looking for your approval
And want to know that you care.
And if they need to talk to you,
To know that you'll be there.

Promises made, or broken
May have had nothing to do with you,
But, it doesn't mean forsake your children
'Cause **you**'ve got a job to do.

Now, about this next commitment,
God is surely taking note.
You may not become the "Dad of the month"
But, you've certainly got my vote.

Please be patient with Mom who's standing by,
As she observes the things you do.
Remember, each time a promise was broken,
She was disappointed too.

She may not have too much to say,
Or seldom wear a smile;
Because of past experience, you may have to
  prove that you're sincere.
And that may take a little while.

~ Patience is a virtue. ~

Dad note: Starting   fresh,   or   starting   new?
Remember, Dad it's up to you.

Reminiscing -
(from one loving mother of the children)

Now, Dad, when I think of you
These words come to mind:
Integrity, fidelity, faithful,
You were most sincere and kind.

That's my ideal, and how it was
When you said that you were mine.
So whether we get back together, or not,
I'm sure things will work out fine.

It's the children we're concerned about now--
For "we" have nothing but time.

~

Dad Scenarios - a team effort

If you had five boys, you might teach them
Basketball, and might score a winning team.
But, with only one lovely daughter,
You might encourage her to live her dream.

Or, you could teach her how to hit a ball
And she might eventually get a homerun.
Anything's possible with skill development
For a father who spends quality time with —
a daughter, or son.

Fatherhood - a Team Effort

Fatherhood is a team effort and presents
A great opportunity for men to shine.
But, it's a big responsibility,
And some things take time.

So if you want to do a great job,
You shouldn't tackle it alone.
Invite Jesus be on your team, then
Make Him Lord of your home.

With God as your captain, no matter what
Your position, He'll keep you in the zone.
You'll stay on course, and never strike out;
He'll always help you win.

Who says you can't do it?
Oh, yes, I know you can!
And if your first try doesn't work,
Be sure to try again.

Let the King of all Kings rule and reign in your heart today, and be led by (His) Holy Spirit...for God is love, and Love never fails.

~

Standing on God's Word:

God's Word says:
(Therefore, I say what His Word says about me):

-   "I can do all things through Christ, who strengtheneth me" (Philippians 4:13). So I say: "I can do all things through Christ, who strengthens me."

-   "If God is for us, who can be against us?" (Romans 8:31b). You can say: "If God is for me, it doesn't matter who's against me."

-   "In all things we are more than conquerors through Him that loved us" (Romans 8:37b). You can say: "I am more than a conqueror."

-   "God is our refuge and strength, a very present help in trouble" (Psalm 46:1). You can say: "God is my refuge and strength, a very present help in trouble."

-   "And the peace of God, which passeth all understanding, shall keep your hearts and minds through Christ Jesus" (Philippians 4:7) You can say: "I have the peace of God that passes all understanding."

~

A Great Man Positioned to Succeed

A Great Man in Position to Succeed:

On your mark! Get ready! Set! Go!!! Let us be your "amen corner." We're so proud of you, because you took the time to read this book and you're almost done. We love you, Dad.

Take Your Position Dad...
... for You are a **Great Man**

Go ahead and take your position. It's one of great authority, because your son needs you to be a role model, and your daughter needs to know how to be respected by a man.

You were meant to be your child's first teacher. So go on and teach! The lessons you share may affect him (her) in an area no one else can reach.

~

"Children, obey your parents in the Lord; for this is right" (Ephesians 6:1).

(You Are) A Great Man!

Don't wait for someone else to tell you,
You've got to know it for yourself.
Deep down inside is a really great man
(You) Might have to pull him off the shelf.

Dust him off. Be real with him.
And always speak the truth.
Remember, no one's perfect.
You may have made a few mistakes.

But, time is of the essence,
So do whatever it takes
Start today, and do the best you can
To become the great man –
your chosen destiny.

Building Character with Words:

- Praise goes a long way, and can do wonders for your children. Let them know that you value them and are happy to have them in your life.

- One encouraging word from you may be the only kind word spoken to your child all day.

- If you can't think of anything positive to say, say "I love you," and know that a smile, and a hug are always welcomed.

~

For the son or daughter who has never experienced the love of a father:

It's important for them to know that they are loved, and that our Heavenly Father loves them more than they'll ever know.

A Special Note to Dads all over the world:

Wherever You Are, Please Dad. . .

Make an effort to spend quality time with your child. Remember, your children are your miracle of life. God equipped you with all of the tools you need to be a great father. You must give of your time, and add to it unconditional love - loving your child in word and deed.

And always find something positive to say, like "There's my shining star," "Hope you had a great day."

On occasion you'll find that child will come to you, when he needs to express himself, whether lonesome, sad or simply feeling blue.

There's no need to look back, only time to improve; and to help your child understand, that you had a lot to do with his pleasant personality - and those strange habits too. :)

We love you Dad, just for being you.

~

Helping Dad Stay in Position

For the mommies who are reading this book too, this page is for you. :)

Mom, if you know that your child's dad is a very good father, and desires to have a strong role in your child's life, please work out your differences so that your child has quality time with him. Children need their dads, too. It was ordained by God. Dads provide protection and security in a natural way. It's is difficult enough for children not to have physical access to both Mom and Dad every day.

One word to the wise woman with children: never degrade or bash your child's father in the presence of your child. If you cannot exonerate, edify or uplift his character, then it is better to remain silent.

Learn to respect one another despite any differences you might have - especially in front of the children - because they are watching. Have respect even when the children are not around. It's so much healthier to get along and to be at peace with one another.

Gone, But Not Forgotten

Death is a part of life, and your child needs to know that. Please show kindness in your actions toward that son or daughter who may have lost a father or mother.

Remember, these dear children will never hear their parent's voice again. Reach out, if you can.

~

Let the orphan, homeless, or fatherless child, who may have experienced the loss of a father through death:

Let them know that God desires to, and would love to be their best, best friend forever, that they can talk to Him; for He's available day or night, and wants to hear from them.

~

Dad, You Left. . .

Dad, you left me and you've gone so far away. The problem isn't that you left, but, that you've gone to stay.

And where you've gone, I can't touch you or see your smile. They say it's close to permanent, that you'll be there for awhile.

No more movies, matinees, or sharing Sunday brunch. No more cookouts, fancy dinners or meeting you for lunch.

You won't be at graduation, won't flip (turn) any more water jugs. Won't hear you say you love me again, or get another hug.

There are some things I'd like to say to you like, "Forgive me for yesterday." "Dad, I promise you I'll do right this time," and "Yes, I'm going to pray."

Tell me why you had to leave? You didn't even say good-bye. Wonder if I'll ever get over this? All I do is cry.

It's not easy, but, I know I must bid you fare well, and say good-bye.

87

What Would Dad Say?

- Dad would want you to know the following:

One day you're gonna' leave here son,
It's just we don't know when.

So the most important thing you can do is
Live life! Have faith in God, and always be kind.
And fill your life with no regrets,
Until He says it's time.

For tomorrow isn't promised to anyone.
Oh, it has nothing to do with age.
That day will come just as sure as you're born,
It's just we don't know when.

To the great dads reading this book:

Maybe you know a child who has lost their father. Maybe there's a niece, nephew, or little cousin that you could extend kindness to once in awhile. Perhaps, you'll be the one to make him (her) smile - again.

The Stats

The Stats are More Than Mere Facts...
...A Sad Reality for Some!

As it relates to suicide:
- 63% of youth suicides are from fatherless homes (Source: *What Can the Federal Government Do To Decrease Crime and Revitalize Communities? –* U. S. Department of Health, 2010 Census)

With regard to behavioral disorders:
- 85% of all children that exhibit behavioral disorders come from fatherless homes (Source: *What Can the Federal Government Do To Decrease Crime and Revitalize Communities? –* Center for Disease Control)

As it relates to juvenile detention:
- 70% of youths in state-operated institutions come from fatherless homes – 9 times the average. (U.S. Dept. of Justice, Sept. 1988)

- 85% of all youths in prison come from fatherless homes – 20 times the average. (Fulton Co. Georgia, Texas Dept. of Correction)

As it relates to delinquency:
- 33% of all juvenile delinquents have parents who are either divorced or separated and
- 44% have parents who were never married,

In contrast to the previous percentage:
- 13% that come from families in which the biological mother and father are married to

each other. (Wisconsin Dept. of Health and Social Services, April 1994).

As it relates to High school dropouts:
Children with fathers who are involved are:

- 70% less likely to drop out of school
- 40% less likely to repeat a grade in school
- more likely to get A's in school
- more likely to enjoy school and engage in extracurricular activities

Children from fatherless homes make up:

- 75% of all adolescent patients in chemical abuse centers, which is 10 times the average
- 71% of all high school dropouts
- And are twice as likely to drop out of school.
(Source: *What Can the Federal Government Do To Decrease Crime and Revitalize Communities?* - (National Principals Association Report)

As it relates to school performance:
- Children from low-income, two-parent families outperform students from high-income, single-parent homes, two to one. *(One-Parent Families and Their Children, Charles F. Kettering Foundation, 1990).*

As it relates to criminal activity:
- The likelihood that a young male will engage in criminal activity doubles if he is raised without a father and triples if he lives in a neighborhood with a high concentration of

single-parent families. (*Source: A. Anne Hill, June O'Neill, Underclass Behaviors in the United States, CUNY, Baruch College. 1993*)

- Little boys from female-head of households show higher levels of aggression as early as fourth grade in comparison to boys from two-parent (mom and dad) households. (N. Vaden-Kierman, N. Ialongo, J. Pearson, and S. Kellam, "Household Family Structure and Children's Aggressive Behavior, *Journal of Abnormal Child Psychology* 23, no. 5 (1995).

Final Daddy Note:
More than anything I encourage you to trust in the Lord with all of your heart and lean on Him, for He can help you do whatever needs to be done. (That's how my Daddy did it!)

It's good to know that Jesus is the same, yesterday, today and forever!

Some Dads Hear Clearly
(Some fail to communicate)

1. Is your son/daughter communicating with you? ___ Yes. ___ NO. If no. Why not?

_____

_____

_____

2. What is your child saying to you?

_____

_____

_____

_____

3. What have you observed?

_____

_____

_____

4. How do you respond to what you hear (them saying to you) or see them do?

_____

_____

_____

_____

5. How would you define quality time as it relates to your child?

_____

_____

_____

a. What does it mean to have quality time vs. spending time with him or her?

_____

_____

_____

_____

b. How much quality time do you spend with your child?

_____

_____

_____

_____

6. Are you a promise keeper or a teacher?

_____

7. How can I make a positive difference in my child's life?

_____

_____

_____

_____

_____

8. Children and youth do what they see us do and say what they hear us say. List 3

things that you are doing today, that you want to see your children do a year from now:

_____

_____

_____

in ten years:

_____

_____

_____

9. List the action you will take to improve the relationship with your children. What changes in your personal life will you have to make?

_____

_____

_____

_____

10. Are there any other obstacles keeping you from moving forward?

_____

_____

Forgiveness will be the key factor in your releasing the weight of the effects of each obstacle in your life.

Now the healing has begun. Congratulations dad!

Great Organizations for Dads

Consider:

Getting involved in your local PTA Organization

National PTA
1250 N. Pitts Street
Alexandria, VA 22314
(800) 307-4782
(703) 518-1200
Info@pta.org
www.pta.org

WatchD.O.G.S. (Dads of Great Students)
1600 West Sunset Ave., Suite B
Springdale, AR 72762
(888) 540-3647
watchdogs@fathers.com
www.fathers.com/watchdogs

Early Childhood Programs **Pre-K Dads**
Detroit Public Schools Community District

Detroit Public Schools C. D. **PTA Dads**

To order additional books visit our website:

www.Leep4Joy.com

If the local store in your area doesn't have this book visible, please ask for it. If it isn't available yet, kindly ask them to contact us.

Patrice Lee continues to write and publish books. She speaks to corporations, youth groups, at conferences, and seminars; and facilitates workshops for K-12 students, teachers and parent organizations.

If this book has helped you in any way, you may share your comments with us: PatriceALee@gmail.com

More books by Patrice Lee:

"...Overcome Every Obstacle ...and Land on Top"
"Bully Me? . . .NO MORE! ! !" (3rd – 6th grade)
"Bully Me? ...NO MAS!!!" (Spanish Translation)
"Bully Me? . . . Oh NO!!!" a TEEN Resource
"Tips" & *"Tools" for a Safe and Healthy School Year*
"Happy to be Me!" (preschool – 2nd grade)
"My Dad, . . .My Friend" (preschool – 4th grade)
"Mommy, Are You Listening?" -for moms, grandmas
"The Bully Met My Dad!"

About the Author:

Patrice Lee was blessed with two precious gifts, a son and a daughter. Having worked with children in public, private, and choice schools settings, and with youth groups throughout the community, author Lee has observed that the common thread among the children and youth as statistics have shown, is that the greatest percentage of them are growing up in fatherless homes. And it's leaving an indelible mark on society.

86719220R00055

Made in the USA
Lexington, KY
15 April 2018